FOOTBALL SUPERSTARS

LIONESSES
RULE

Hi, pleased to meet you.

We hope you enjoy our book about the Lionesses!

I'm **VARbot** with all the facts and stats!

SIMON   DAN

WELBECK

Published in 2023 by Welbeck Children's Limited,
part of the Welbeck Publishing Group
Offices in: London - 20 Mortimer Street, London W1T 3JW &
Sydney - Level 17, 207 Kent St, Sydney NSW 2000 Australia
www.welbeckpublishing.com
Text © 2023 Simon Mugford
Design & Illustration © 2023 Dan Green
ISBN: 978-1-80453-527-1

Writer: Simon Mugford
Designer and Illustrator: Dan Green
Design Manager: Sam James
Senior Commissioning Editor: Suhel Ahmed
Production: Melanie Robertson
Research Assistant: Eleanor Reid

A catalogue record for this book is available from the British Library.

FSC
www.fsc.org
MIX
Paper | Supporting
responsible forestry
FSC® C171272

Printed in the UK
10 9 8 7 6 5 4 3 2 1

Statistics and records correct as of August 2023

FOOTBALL SUPERSTARS

LIONESSES

RULE

SIMON MUGFORD   DAN GREEN

CONTENTS

INTRODUCTION

Are you a fan of the **ENGLAND Women's football team?** We are! This book is all about the **AMAZING, AWESOME, INCREDIBLE . . .**

LIONESSES!

Learn how England's women footballers overcame bans and prejudice to win millions of fans and eventually become *EUROPEAN CHAMPIONS* . . .

Get the lowdown on your *favourite players* with all the *key facts* and *stats* . . .

Welcome to . . .
LIONESSES RULE!

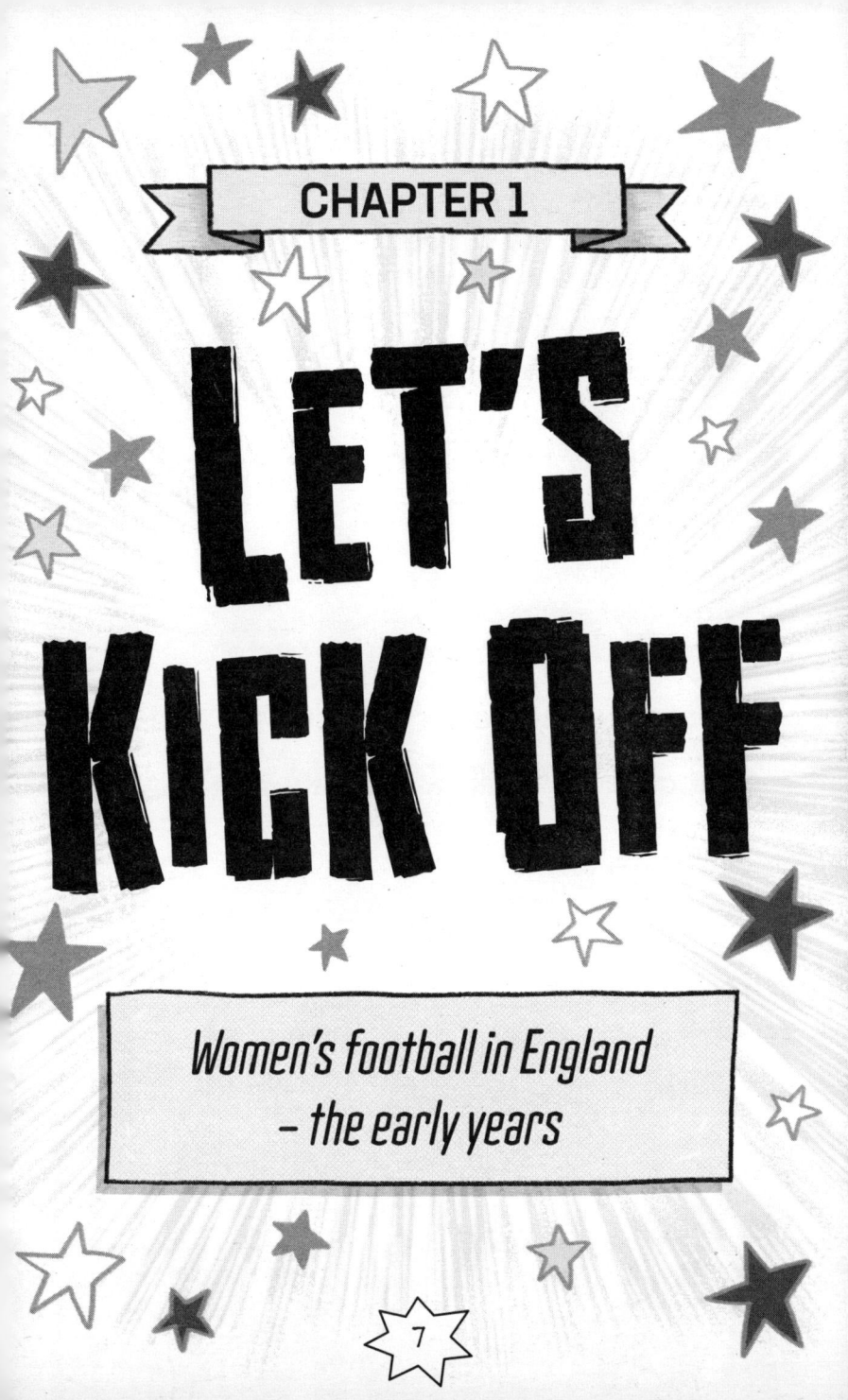

CHAPTER 1

LET'S KICK OFF

Women's football in England
– the early years

THE PIONEERING
DICK, KERR LADIES

In **1917,** millions of British men were fighting in the **First World War.** Women worked in factories.

At the **Dick, Kerr** factory in Preston, Lancashire, the women formed their own football team. **Dick, Kerr Ladies F.C.** played against both men's and women's teams, mainly in the north of England.

8

By **1920,** the team were playing to huge crowds.

30 APRIL 1920

DICK, KERR LADIES 2-0 'FRANCE'

DEEPDALE STADIUM, PRESTON

A team of French women players toured England and played four matches against **Dick, Kerr Ladies** *- aka 'England'. The Preston factory workers won two, drew one and lost one!*

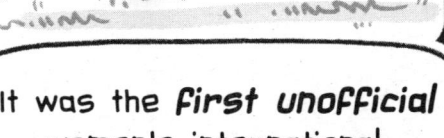

It was the **first unofficial** women's international.

THE INCREDIBLE
LILY PARR

One of the Dick, Kerr Ladies players is a **LEGEND** of the women's game - **Lily Parr.**

Tall and strong, Lily was just 14 when she joined the team. She went on to play more than **400 times** for Dick, Kerr Ladies and is said to have scored more than **900 goals!**

Lily scored **43 goals** in her first season - as a left-back.

NAME: LILY PARR

POSITION: LEFT WINGER / LEFT-BACK / FORWARD

PLAYING YEARS: 1919-1951

ENGLAND **ICON**

11

Dick, Kerr Ladies were **HUGELY** popular. On **Boxing Day 1920,** the team played a charity match against **St Helen's Ladies** at Everton's **Goodison Park** stadium.

A capacity crowd of **53,000** (with thousands locked out) saw **Dick, Kerr Ladies** win 4-0.

This was the biggest attendance for a women's game in England for *98 YEARS!*

But, in 1921, the **MEN** in charge at the **English Football Association** didn't like it. They said the game was "unsuitable for females"!

NO LADIES ALLOWED ON OUR PITCHES!

So they **BANNED** women from playing at its clubs.

The women's teams organised matches themselves! Dick, Kerr Ladies even went on a successful tour of the **USA.**

HOWDY!

Incredibly, the English FA ban on women's football lasted for **50 YEARS.**

There were similar bans in *BRAZIL, GERMANY* and *FRANCE.*

LET US PLAY!

FOOTBALL FOR WOMEN!

NOT FAIR!

Meanwhile, men's football became the

WORLD'S BIGGEST SPORT!

CHAPTER 2

THE GIRLS ARE BACK!

The first Lionesses

By the 1970s, things began to change. After **England's men** had won the **World Cup** in **1966**, football became bigger than ever.

So the FA **FINALLY** lifted its ban in **1971**.

ABOUT TIME!

AT LAST!
What took
so long?

Women Rule!

16

Women's football leagues were formed all over Europe, and in 1971, **France** and the **Netherlands** played the first **OFFICIAL** international football match.

France won 4-0.

THE 'AULD ENEMY'

18 NOVEMBER 1972

INTERNATIONAL FRIENDLY

SCOTLAND 2-3 ENGLAND

RAVENSCRAIG STADIUM, GREENOCK

England women's first **OFFICIAL** international match was against - who else, but **SCOTLAND!**

Scotland in November is **cold!** The ground was **frozen** and by the second half it was **snowing heavily.**

Scotland had a **2–0 lead** before **Sylvia Gore** scored the first **English** international women's goal.

England scored **twice more** for a famous **3–2 win.**

The match took place almost 100 years to the day after the first ever men's international – between *England* and *Scotland.*

FIRST GOALSCORER

As a **Manchester Corinthians** player in the 1950s, **Sylvia Gore** travelled to South America where the team played in front of crowds of up to 80,000. She was only 13!

Before scoring that **historic first goal** for England against Scotland, Sylvia once scored an incredible **143 goals** in a season for Corinthians.

NAME: SYLVIA MARGARET GORE

POSITION: ATTACKING MIDFIELDER

ENGLAND CAREER: 1972-1979

ENGLAND
ICON

21

DAYS OF THUNDER

At **1.52 metres** tall, **Pat Davies** was tiny - especially for a centre-forward. But Pat had a super-powerful shot - she was known as **'Thunder' Davies!**

Pat concentrated on playing for her club, *Southampton*, and only played *seven games* for England. But she scored *10 goals!*

NAME: PAT DAVIES

POSITION: STRIKER

ENGLAND CAREER: 1972-1978

ENGLAND
ICON

BOOM!

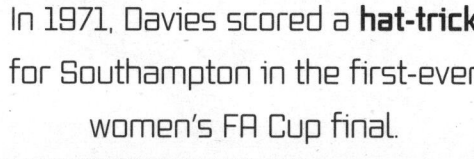

In 1971, Davies scored a **hat-trick** for Southampton in the first-ever women's FA Cup final.

23

POWELL
THE TRAILBLAZER

Hope Powell grew up in south London, where she played football with her stepbrothers in the cages and concrete pitches on the estate where they lived.

She was the best player in her **school team,** where boys and girls played together.

But the FA rules said she had to stop playing in mixed teams when she was **11.**

SOUTH LONDON NEWS

LET HOPE WIN!

Hope protested and it made the news!

But then she found the **Millwall Lionesses** - and never looked back.

NAME: HOPE POWELL

POSITION: MIDFIELDER

ENGLAND CAREER: 1983-1998

CAPS: 66

GOALS: 35

ENGLAND ICON

Hope was a great England player, but as a manager, she did so much for the women's game. Hope was still a **teenager** when she started her coaching qualifications and became the first woman to hold the **UEFA Pro Licence.**

She was the first full-time England coach and the first woman to hold the position.

Hope managed England at **TWO World Cups** and **FOUR EUROs,** taking them to the final at **EURO 2009.**

Hope paved the way for the *success* of the Lionesses today.

"I KNEW AT THE AGE OF 11 THAT I WAS GOOD ENOUGH TO PLAY FOR ENGLAND . . . I WAS BETTER THAN EVERY BOY ON MY ESTATE AND EVERY BOY I PLAYED AGAINST."

Hope Powell.

CHAPTER 3

THE LEGENDS

The great Lionesses from the past

FARA WILLIAMS

POSITION: MIDFIELDER

CAPS: 172

GOALS: 40

ENGLAND CAREER: 2001-2019

At the age of 18, Fara found herself **homeless,** but with the support of her coaches at **Everton** and **England,** she went on to captain both her club and country. Fara played at three **World Cups,** and earned a **third-place** finish in 2015.

ICONIC FACT

 Fara is England's most-capped player of all time in both the women's and men's teams.

KELLY SMITH

POSITION: STRIKER

CAPS: 117

GOALS: 46

ENGLAND CAREER: 1995-2014

A true Lioness legend, Kelly Smith is one of the best strikers in the history of the women's game. Blessed with speed, agility, and a **magic first touch,** she made her name playing in the **USA** before winning multiple trophies with **Arsenal.**

ICONIC FACT

With 46 goals, Kelly is England's second-highest scorer (after Ellen White).

ALEX SCOTT

POSITION: DEFENDER

CAPS: 140

GOALS: 12

ENGLAND CAREER: 2004-2017

Fierce, strong and full of pace, Alex was **THE** number one England right-back of her time. Scouted by Arsenal when she was just eight, Alex became club captain in 2014. She played in **four EUROs, three World Cups** and the **2012 London Olympics.**

ICONIC FACT

Now a TV pundit and presenter, Alex competed on the 2019 series of Strictly Come Dancing!

KAREN BARDLSEY

POSITION: *GOALKEEPER*

CAPS: *82*

GOALS: *–*

ENGLAND CAREER: *2005-2022*

'KB' was born in **California** (her mum and dad are English) and began her career in the USA before moving to **Europe.** A commanding figure in goal, Karen represented England at **seven major** tournaments and for Team GB at the 2012 Olympics.

ICONIC FACT

Bardsley played in three of the biggest leagues in the world: England's WSL, America's NWSL and Sweden's Damallsvenskan.

MARY PHILLIP

POSITION: DEFENDER

CAPS: 65

GOALS: 0

ENGLAND CAREER: 1995-2008

A native south Londoner, Mary toughed it out as a kid, playing football with her brothers. She was a Lioness with **Millwall** before playing for England, where she became the **first black woman** to wear the England captain's armband.

ICONIC FACT

Mary was four months pregnant when she was called up for the World Cup in 1995.

RACHEL YANKEY

POSITION: MIDFIELDER / FORWARD

CAPS: 129

GOALS: 19

ENGLAND CAREER: 1997-2013

Yankey's backstory reads like a movie script – she **shaved her hair short** and **pretended to be a boy** named 'Ray' so she could play football! The Arsenal winger went on to play 129 times for England, at one point being her country's most-capped player.

ICONIC FACT

 Rachel made her England debut against Scotland aged 18 – and scored!

CASEY STONEY

POSITION: DEFENDER

CAPS: 130

GOALS: 6

ENGLAND CAREER: 2000-2017

Casey was a key player at **EURO 2009** and the **2007 World Cup** before captaining Team GB at the 2012 Olympics.

ENIOLA ALUKO

POSITION: FORWARD

CAPS: 105

GOALS: 33

ENGLAND CAREER: 2000-2017

Now a familiar face as a TV sports broadcaster, Aluko played in the **US, Italy** and **England.** She was the **joint top-scorer** in qualifying for the **2015 World Cup.**

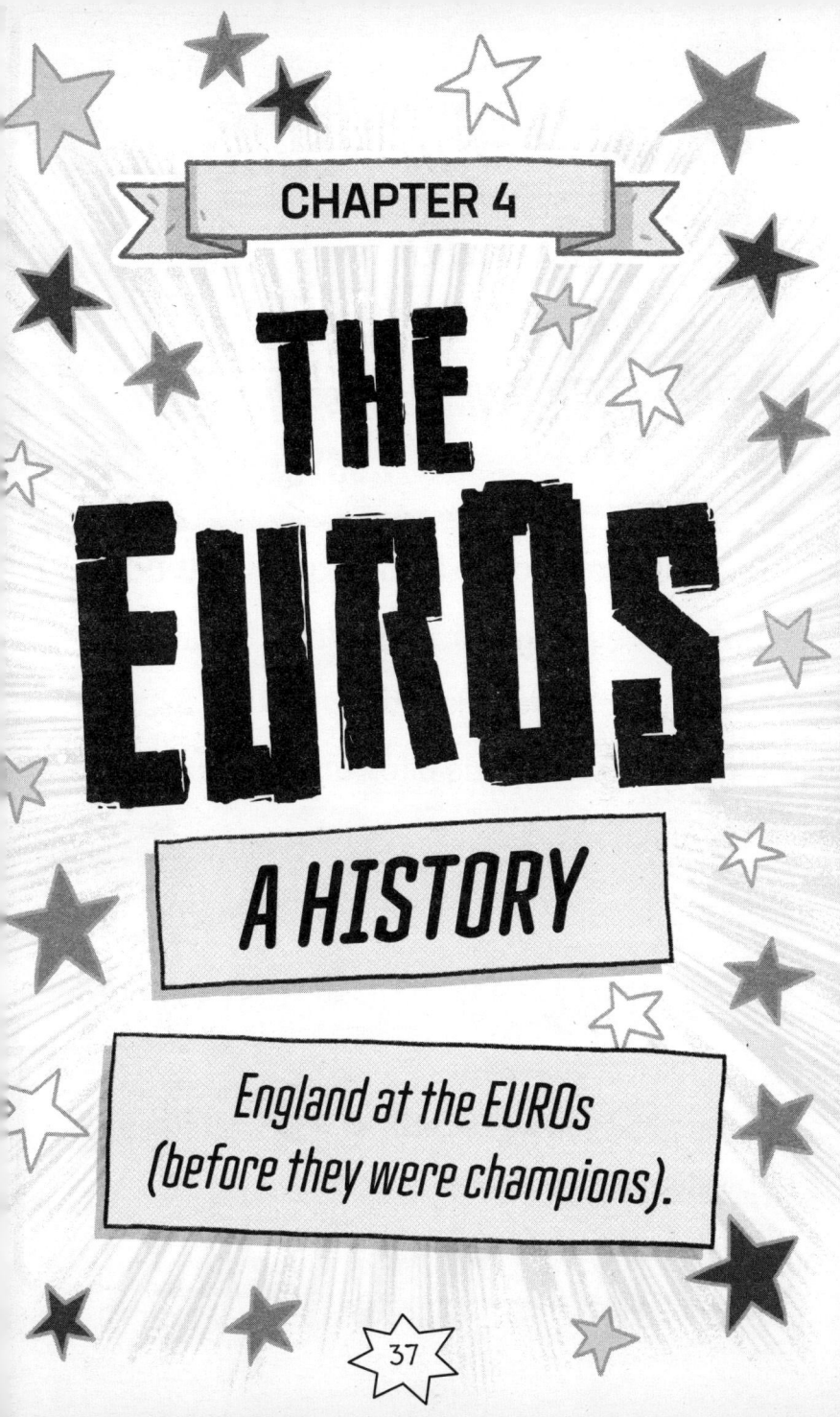

CHAPTER 4

THE EUROS

A HISTORY

England at the EUROs
(before they were champions).

PENALTY PAIN – EURO 1984

CHAMPIONS: SWEDEN

ENGLAND POSITION: RUNNERS-UP

FINAL ATTENDANCES: 5,662 1ST LEG
2,567 2ND LEG

England reached the final - against **Sweden** - which was played over two legs. Ending 1-1 on aggregate, England lost the **penalty shoot-out** on a very muddy pitch at Kenilworth Road.

EURO FACT

The matches were played with a smaller ball and lasted only 70 minutes!

NORTHERN LIGHTS – EURO 1987

CHAMPIONS: NORWAY

ENGLAND POSITION: FOURTH PLACE

FINAL ATTENDANCE: 8,408

In a repeat of the 1984 final, **England** faced **Sweden** in the semi-final, this time losing 3-2 and ultimately finishing fourth after a play-off with Italy.

Kerry Davis

EURO FACT

England beat Northern Ireland 10-0 in qualifying!

GERMANY RULE! – EURO 1995

CHAMPIONS: GERMANY

ENGLAND POSITION: SEMI-FINALIST

FINAL ATTENDANCE: 8,500

England had failed to qualify for the three previous EUROs (in 1989, '91 and '93). This time, they were totally outclassed by Germany (led by the legendary **Birgit Prinz**), losing 6-2 over the two-legged semi-final.

 EURO FACT

This was the third time Germany had won the tournament.

Birgit Prinz

DISAPPOINTMENT – *EURO 2001*

CHAMPIONS: GERMANY

ENGLAND POSITION: GROUP STAGE

FINAL ATTENDANCE: 18,000

For the first time, England were in a tournament of **eight teams** instead of four. Sadly, they could only manage to **draw** with Russia - with Angela Banks scoring for England - before they lost to both Sweden and eventual champions Germany.

Angela Banks

EURO FACT

Germany won the final with a 'Golden Goal' - a rule where the team that scored first in extra time won the match.

HOME DISADVANTAGE – *EURO 2005*

CHAMPIONS: *GERMANY*

ENGLAND POSITION: *GROUP STAGE*

FINAL ATTENDANCE: *21,105*

England hosted a brilliant tournament, with **record crowds** and matches shown on **TV.** Unfortunately, they couldn't match the success on the pitch.

EURO FACT

29,092 fans saw England beat Finland 3-2 (their only win) at the City of Manchester Stadium - a EUROs record for a women's match at the time.

BACK AND BETTER – EURO 2009

CHAMPIONS: GERMANY (YES, AGAIN)

ENGLAND POSITION: RUNNERS-UP

FINAL ATTENDANCE: 15,877

England squeaked through the group stage, then beat the hosts **Finland** and the **Netherlands** to reach a first final since 1984. Unfortunately, they faced the mighty Germany in the final and were beaten 6-2.

EURO FACT

Jill Scott played in her FIRST EUROs final at this tournament . . .

Jill Scott

43

LEARNING CURVE – EURO 2013

CHAMPIONS: GERMANY *(YEP!)*

ENGLAND POSITION: GROUP STAGE

FINAL ATTENDANCE: 41,301

Women's football was finally getting the support it deserved - **more people** watched EURO 2013 than any of the previous EURO Championships. However, despite **Laura Bassett's** first England goal, against Spain, England failed to improve on their 2009 final placing. Time for a reset!

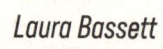

Laura Bassett

EURO FACT

This was the first Women's EUROs with an official anthem – "Winning Ground" sung by Swedish pop star Eric Saade.

LOOK TO THE FUTURE – *EURO 2017*

CHAMPIONS: NETHERLANDS

ENGLAND POSITION: SEMI-FINALISTS

FINAL ATTENDANCE: 28,182

An expanded tournament featuring **16 teams** saw a much-improved England reach the semi-final, thanks to top scorer Jodie Taylor. They were beaten by the excellent Netherlands side coached by future Lionesses boss **Sarina Wiegman.**

Jodie Taylor

EURO FACT

England beat France for the first time in 43 years in the quarter-final.

"WE SCORED A LOT OF GOALS, PLAYED SOME GREAT FOOTBALL . . . WE'LL COME BACK STRONGER NEXT TIME"

Lucy Bronze on England's EURO 2017 performance.

OUT NOW!

BRONZE RULES

46

CHAPTER 5

HOW TO BE A LIONESS

SQUAD GOALS

In England, we're very lucky to have the Lionesses - one of the **best** international women's teams in the world.

How does a super team like the Lionesses work together? What are their different roles on the pitch?

48

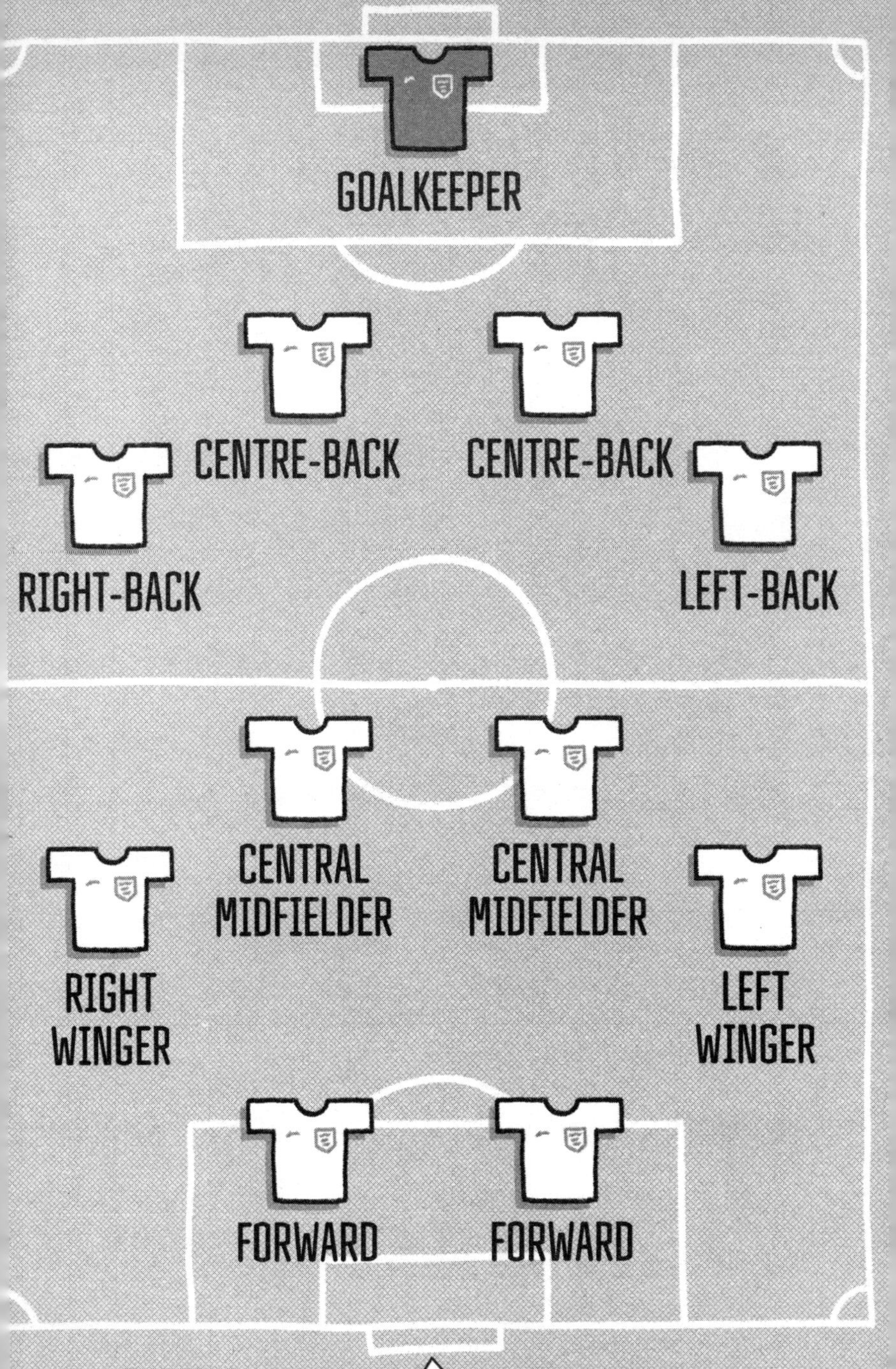

GOALKEEPER

CENTRE-BACK   CENTRE-BACK

RIGHT-BACK   LEFT-BACK

CENTRAL   CENTRAL
MIDFIELDER   MIDFIELDER

RIGHT   LEFT
WINGER   WINGER

FORWARD   FORWARD

AT THE BACK – DEFENDERS

Defenders rarely get the glory that creative midfielders and strikers get. But their job is **ESSENTIAL** for a winning team.

Defenders need to be **strong,** with **quick reactions** and superb **heading skills.** They also need to be fearless when going in for a tackle!

FWOMP!

50

Millie Bright excels in England's defence.

SAFE HANDS – THE GOALKEEPER

Keepers are **UNIQUE** in many ways. They wear a different coloured strip and different rules apply to them. Keepers are heroes when they make an  awesome save, as they are a team's last line of defence.

If you want to be a goalkeeper, you need to **stay alert** for the whole game, talk to (and sometimes shout at) your team-mates and of course, be **super-agile** so you can dive and make those all-important saves.

HEART OF THE ACTION – MIDFIELDERS

Midfield players have different roles according to their position or style of play. Some play an **attacking role,** while others are **more defensive**.

All midfielders need to be ready to do both!

Midfielders usually have the most possession and **do the most running**! They often assist with goals, though some of the best attacking midfielders score a lot, too.

ZOOM!

Georgia Stanway plays mostly as an attacking midfielder.

GOAL GETTERS - STRIKERS

Goalscorers are usually the most prized players in a team. Midfielders and defenders contribute goals of course, but the all-out striker has a single aim - **scoring goals.**

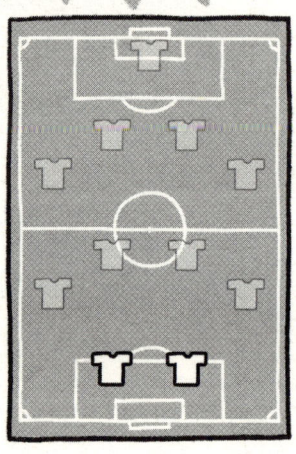

Some strikers use **strength and height** to beat their opponents, while others rely on **speed, dribbling** and **ball skills.** All strikers need the vision to spot a goalscoring opportunity and put themselves in a position to make that shot!

Beth Mead – a natural goalscorer.

KA-POW!

THE ONE IN CHARGE - MANAGER

It's tough being a football manager! Their job is to **select the team,** give **instructions** and **support** their players to perform at the highest level.

A team's **style and attitude,** and the way they approach a game all start with the manager.

Why do managers wear two watches?

In case they need extra time.

SUPPORT – BACKROOM STAFF

It's not just the players who are part of the Lionesses squad. There's a whole team of backroom staff – **coaches, physios, kit managers,**

chefs, coach-drivers and others who are all there to support the manager and the players.

60

CHAPTER 6

QUEENS OF EUROPE

The story of EURO 2022

IT'S COMING **HOME!**

As the host nation, England was **MASSIVELY** excited about **EURO 2022!**

The fans even had to wait an extra year because of the *Covid pandemic.*

England were drawn in a group with **Austria, Northern Ireland** and **Norway.**

 ENGLAND

 AUSTRIA

 NORWAY

 NORTHERN IRELAND

NORTHERN IRELAND

The team would play all over the country, from venues in **Manchester** to **Brighton,** and **Southampton** to **Sheffield.**

Millions more would watch the matches on the TV . . .

COME ON ENGLAND!

LIONESSES

63

IN THE **GROUP STAGE**

England began the
tournament against
Austria at Old Trafford.
It was nervy and tense
until - **BOOM!** - Beth Mead
scored after **16 minutes**

and the team held on for a **1-0** victory.

Next up, **Norway** - England's semi-final
opponents in the previous two tournaments.
Incredibly, this time round the Scandinavians
were blown away and beaten **8-0!**

Beth Mead scored
a *hat-trick!*

England finished the group stage with another **BIG** win - **5–0** against Northern Ireland.

20 JULY 2022

EURO 2022 QUARTER-FINAL

ENGLAND 2-1 SPAIN (AET)

BRIGHTON & HOVE COMMUNITY STADIUM, BRIGHTON

England went into this match having scored **14 goals** and conceded none. So it was a shock when **Spain** went ahead early in the second half.

Ella Toone's late equaliser forced extra-time before **Georgia Stanway's** thunderous winner sent the fans wild!

The Lionesses had shown their strength – and **roared** into the semi-finals!

26 JULY 2022

EURO 2022 SEMI-FINAL

ENGLAND 4-0 SWEDEN

BRAMALL LANE, SHEFFIELD

Opponents **Sweden** were finalists at the **Tokyo Olympics** in 2021 – a strong team!

Who else but **Beth Mead** opened the scoring, before **Lucy Bronze, Alessia Russo** (a cheeky backheel) and **Fran Kirby** made it **FOUR** to cap off an incredible, historic victory.

WEMBLEY HERE WE GO!

CHAMPIONS OF EUROPE

31 JULY 2022

EURO 2022 FINAL

ENGLAND 2-1 GERMANY (AET)

WEMBLEY STADIUM

It doesn't get much bigger than England versus **Germany** – at Wembley. Germany had won this competition **EIGHT** times already!

The game was goalless until **Ella Toone** (who had just come off the bench) put the Lionesses ahead on 62 minutes. But this was Germany, and they made it **1–1** with 11 minutes to go, forcing the match into extra time.

The attendance was **87,192** – a record EUROS final crowd for men OR women.

A packed Wembley watched nervously as both sides had good chances and then . . . **Chloe Kelly** wrote herself into the history books with her **110th minute goal!**

YES!

CHAMPIONS – AT LAST!

"NEVER FORGET WHERE YOU COME FROM. WE KNOW IT WILL CHANGE FOR THE TEAM FROM THIS MOMENT BUT NEVER FORGET THE GENERATION BEFORE."

Sarina Wiegman, after the famous EURO 2022 win.

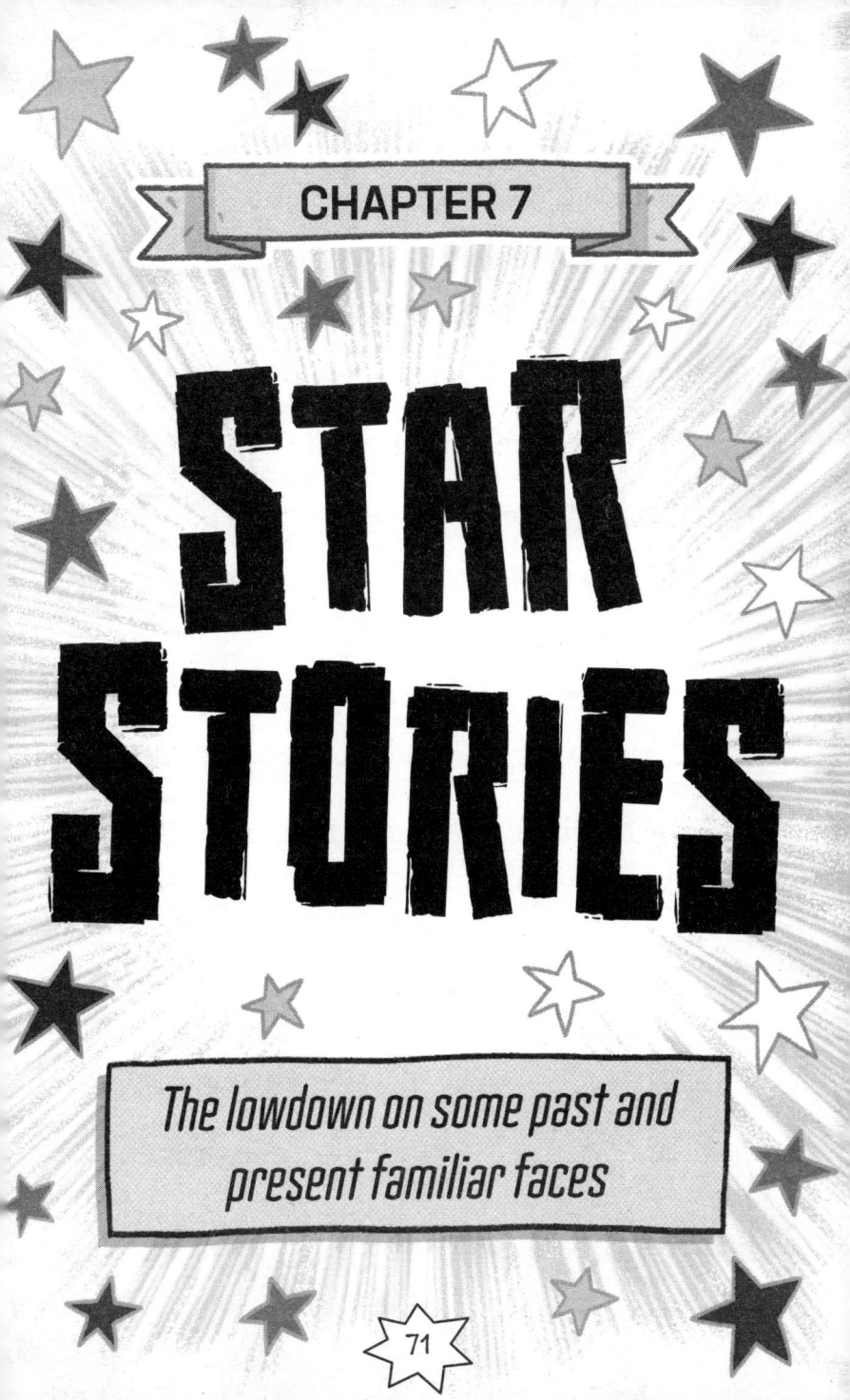

CHAPTER 7

STAR STORIES

The lowdown on some past and present familiar faces

THE *WHITE* STUFF

Ellen White grew up in a **football-mad** family. She started out playing for a local team where her dad was a coach.

BOP!

Scouted by **Arsenal** aged just **EIGHT,** Ellen made headlines when she was **BANNED** from playing in her local league - because she was a girl. **NOT FAIR!**

Fast forward to the **2019 World Cup,** where the then **Man City** striker's 'goggles' celebration made her a global star!

In 2021, Ellen scored a **hat-trick** in a 20-0 victory over Latvia, to smash Kelly Smith's record and become England's all-time record goalscorer.

ELLEN WHITE

POSITION: FORWARD

CAPS: 113

GOALS: 52

YEARS: 2010-2022

ENGLAND ICON

TOUGH ENOUGH

Lucy Bronze's middle name is **Tough** and she certainly lives up to it!

She was **VERY** competitive as a little girl, never afraid to get stuck into whichever sport she played, especially football.

Lucy once tackled a **boy** she was playing against so hard, she made him cry!

Today, the multiple award – and trophy – winner

is a truly world-class player. She

famously scored two crucial (and

almost identical) goals against

Norway in the quarter-finals

of both the **2015** and **2019**

World Cups.

BLAM!

LUCY BRONZE

POSITION: DEFENDER

CAPS: 112

GOALS: 12

CLUB: BARCELONA

ENGLAND
ICON

THE NEED FOR MEAD

Beth Mead played lots of sports as a kid, but **football** was her first - and biggest - love. With her blonde hair in a ponytail, she easily **stood out** as the only girl playing in the boys' teams.

TAKE THAT BOYS!

The boys **teased her** and called her names, but the young Beth soon shut them up by scoring **goals** - lots of them. And it's continued ever since!

The fast, athletic striker was the **standout star** of EURO 2022. Named player of the tournament, her six goals also won her the **Golden Boot.** Sadly, Beth was unfortunate to miss the **2023 World Cup** due to injury.

BETH MEAD

POSITION: FORWARD

CAPS: 50

GOALS: 29

CLUB: ARSENAL

ENGLAND ICON

CAPTAIN AND QUEEN

Leah Williamson was born into football rivalry - half her family are **Tottenham** fans, while the other half support **Arsenal,** where she has played since she was **NINE.**

She nearly decided to try for a career in **athletics,** but thankfully for England fans she switched to football, where she's become born leader, with superb tactical skills and passing abilities.

As the captain of England, Leah lifted the EURO 2022 trophy after playing **every minute of every game** at the tournament. Unfortunately, Leah was injured for the 2023 World Cup.

LEAH WILLIAMSON

POSITION: DEFENDER

CAPS: 43

GOALS: 4

CLUB: ARSENAL

ENGLAND **ICON**

JILL SCOTT

Jill Scott started out as a long-distance runner before making her name as a player with hometown club **Sunderland.** She went on to play for **Everton** and **Manchester City.**

Jill was a **massive character** on and off the pitch – she made sure everyone in the dressing room was fired up for a match.

Shortly after the **EURO 2022** win, Jill famously won **'I'm a Celebrity... Get Me Out of Here'!**

80

Representing England at no fewer than **EIGHT** major tournaments, and now a hugely popular **TV pundit,** Jill is a genuine **Lioness legend.**

JILL SCOTT

POSITION: MIDFIELDER

CAPS: 161

GOALS: 27

YEARS: 2006-2022

NATIONAL TREASURE

"IF YOU WOULD HAVE TOLD ME THAT I'D LIVE TO SEE 90,000 PEOPLE PACKED INTO WEMBLEY STADIUM FOR A WOMEN'S EUROPEAN FINAL? AND THAT I'D BE PLAYING IN IT? IMPOSSIBLE."

Jill Scott

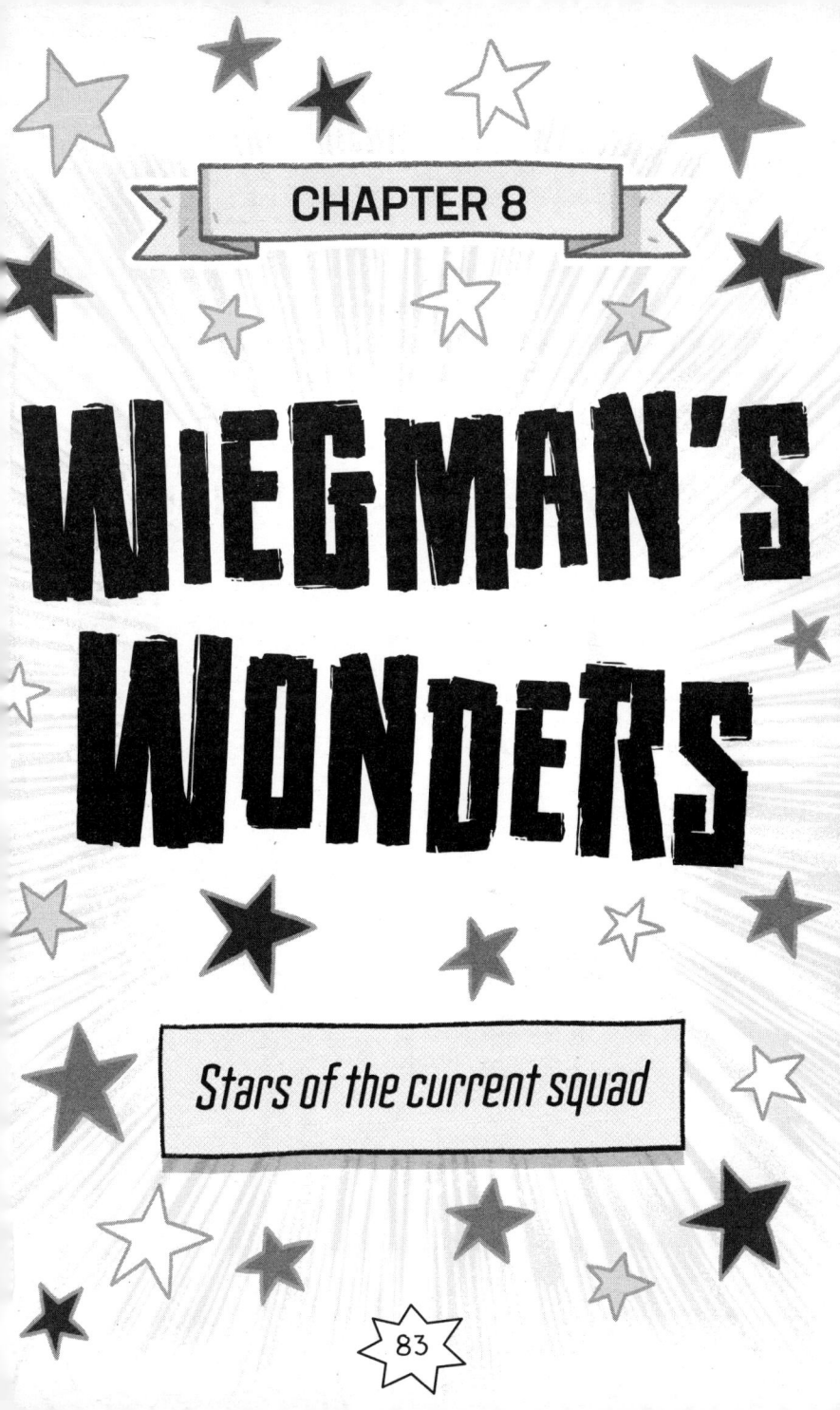

MILLIE BRIGHT

POSITION: DEFENDER

CAPS: 73

GOALS: 5

CLUB: MANCHESTER CITY

*Strong and physical, Bright's presence and **domination** in the air is key to England's defence. England's vice-captain has proved her worth as a goalscorer, too, becoming **joint-top scorer** in the **2022 Arnold Clark trophy.***

ALEX GREENWOOD

POSITION: DEFENDER

CAPS: 82

GOALS: 5

CLUB: MANCHESTER CITY

Always recognisable by her **distinctive eyelashes,** Greenwood is a defender who likes to get forward and support the attack. Something of a legend in **north-west England,** Alex has played for Everton, Liverpool and Man United as well as City!

GEORGIA STANWAY

POSITION: MIDFIELDER

CAPS: 56

GOALS: 16

CLUB: BAYERN MUNICH

*Stanway is full of energy, beating her opponents with strength and speed. She's scored some memorable goals from **long-range,** including her **stunning winner** in extra-time against Spain in the **EURO 2022** quarter-final.*

ELLA TOONE

POSITION: MIDFIELDER

CAPS: 38

GOALS: 17

CLUB: MANCHESTER UNITED

Lively and entertaining both on and off the pitch, Toone is skilled at creating chances and setting up her team-mates. She's also not afraid to **shoot from distance** and has become a regular scorer under Sarina Wiegman.

CHLOE KELLY

POSITION: FORWARD

CAPS: 32

GOALS: 7

CLUB: MANCHESTER CITY

*Londoner Kelly grew up playing football with her **FIVE brothers**, before working her way up through the England set-up. She made history by scoring the **winner** in the **EURO 2022 final** and gained worldwide fame for that iconic celebration!*

KEIRA WALSH

POSITION: MIDFIELDER

CAPS: 65

GOALS: 0

CLUB: BARCELONA

England's playmaker is **ESSENTIAL** to the team's success, but Walsh's low-key contributions can sometimes be overlooked. Barcelona noticed her though, paying a world record **£400,000** to sign her in 2022.

ALESSIA RUSSO

POSITION: FORWARD

CAPS: 28

GOALS: 14

CLUB: ARSENAL

*Goals seem to come easily for Russo – she scored a hat-trick in just 11 minutes against Latvia – the fastest Lioness hat-trick on record, and famously, that incredible, **cheeky back-heeled goal** in the EURO 2022 semi-final.*

FRAN KIRBY

POSITION: MIDFIELDER

CAPS: 65

GOALS: 17

CLUB: CHELSEA

*The small but mighty Kirby is Chelsea's **all-time top goalscorer** and is a key member of the team that has come to dominate the WSL. Fran fought illness to play at EURO 2022, Where she was a key contributor, but she missed the **2023 World Cup** with an injury.*

91

MARY EARPS

POSITION: GOALKEEPER

CAPS: 40

CLEAN SHEETS: 24

CLUB: MANCHESTER UNITED

England's number one **between the sticks** is an avid TikToker - with more than **650,000 followers.**

BETHANY ENGLAND

POSITION: FORWARD

CAPS: 25

GOALS: 11

CLUB: TOTTENHAM HOSTPUR

The suitably-named England is an **awesome attacking force,** but can also play in midfield and even at the back if necessary.

JESS CARTER

POSITION: DEFENDER

CAPS: 23

GOALS: 1

CLUB: CHELSEA

*Since debuting in the **Champions League** with Birmingham City aged 16, the young defender is now firmly a part of the England squad.*

LOTTE WUBBEN-MOY

POSITION: DEFENDER

CAPS: 10

GOALS: 0

CLUB: ARSENAL

*A key Lioness squad member, Lotte is active in speaking out on **equality issues** - especially in football.*

RACHEL DALY

POSITION: DEFENDER

CAPS: 75

GOALS: 14

CLUB: ASTON VILLA

Daly is a very adaptable player and played as an **attacker** in her eight years with **Houston Dash** in the USA.

LAUREN JAMES

POSITION: DEFENDER

CAPS: 15

GOALS: 4

CLUB: CHELSEA

Lauren came through England's **youth set up** and earned a reputation as one of the best young players at the **2023 World Cup**.

JORDAN NOBBS

POSITION: MIDFIELDER

CAPS: 71

GOALS: 8

CLUB: ASTON VILLA

Jordan missed both the **2019 World Cup** and **EURO 2022** due to injury, but has fought her way back to the Lionesses squad

LAUREN HEMP

POSITION: FORWARD

CAPS: 45

GOALS: 13

CLUB: MANCHESTER CITY

Four-times winner of the **PFA Young Player of the Year,** Hemp is one of England's brightest young talents.

NIAMH CHARLES

POSITION: DEFENDER

CAPS: 7

GOALS: 0

CLUB: CHELSEA

*Versatile and quick, Charles worked hard to win a place in the **2023 World Cup squad**.*

NIKITA PARRIS

POSITION: FORWARD

CAPS: 71

GOALS: 17

CLUB: MANCHESTER UNITED

*Liverpool-born Nikita formed her **own girls football team** when she was just 11 - and they went on to win their league!*

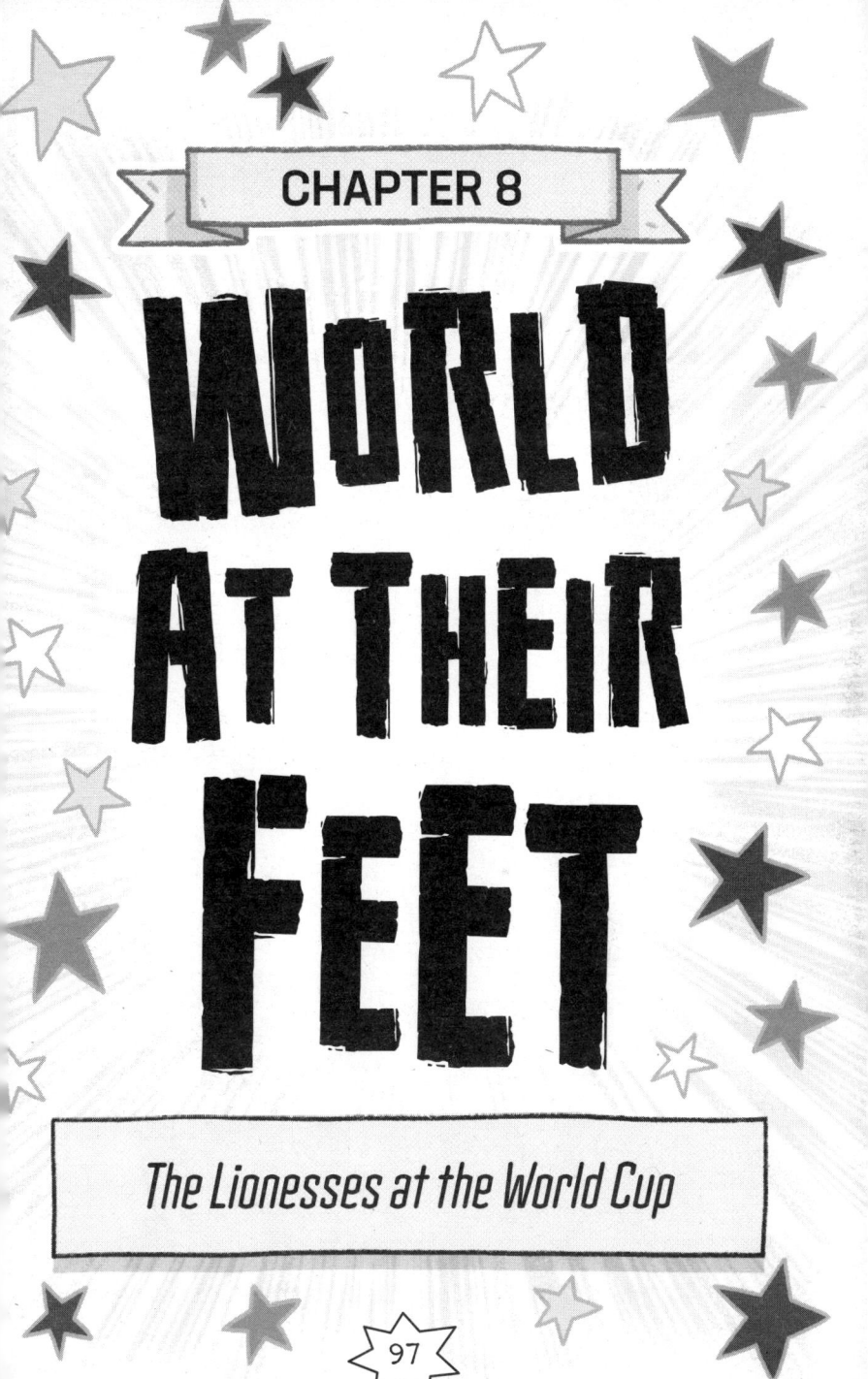

CHAPTER 8

WORLD AT THEIR FEET

The Lionesses at the World Cup

A STRONG START – 1995

HOST NATION: SWEDEN

CHAMPIONS: NORWAY

ENGLAND POSITION: QUARTER-FINALIST

The **second edition** of the Women's World Cup was England's first. Their only group-stage defeat was to eventual champions **Norway,** and the Lionesses' tournament was ended by old rivals **Germany,** 3-0 in the quarter-final.

WORLD CUP FACT

This World Cup was originally going to be held in Bulgaria.

EASTERN PROMISE – 2007

HOST NATION: CHINA
CHAMPIONS: GERMANY
ENGLAND POSITION: QUARTER-FINALIST

England travelled to China for their first **World Cup** in 12 years. They held eventual winners **Germany to a 0–0 draw** and celebrated an excellent 6-1 win over Argentina. But the **USA** proved too strong as the Lionesses suffered another quarter-final exit.

WORLD CUP FACT

None of the knockout matches went to extra time at this tournament.

FEELING THE BLUES – 2011

HOST NATION: GERMANY

CHAMPIONS: JAPAN

ENGLAND POSITION: QUARTER-FINALIST

England topped their group where they actually **BEAT** the ultimate winners Japan, but the adventure ended with a third straight **quarter-final exit.** Jill Scott gave the Lionesses the lead against France, but they equalised and won a penalty shoot-out.

WORLD CUP FACT

England and Brazil did not lose a game but went home after losing quarter-final penalty shoot-outs.

SEMI-SUCCESSFUL – 2015

HOST NATION: CANADA
CHAMPIONS: USA
ENGLAND POSITION: THIRD PLACE

England reached the round of 16 where **Lucy Bronze's** stunner knocked out **Norway.** A brilliant win over hosts Canada took the Lionesses to their **first-ever semi-final.** There, reigning champions Japan were too strong for England, but there was the consolation of a win over Germany to claim **third place.**

WORLD CUP FACT

This edition was bigger than before, with 24 teams in the finals instead of 16.

PUSHING ON – 2019

HOST NATION: FRANCE

CHAMPIONS: USA

ENGLAND POSITION: FOURTH PLACE

The Lionesses squad was becoming familiar to fans. England were free-scoring and fiery, with the likes of **Steph Houghton, Alex Greenwood** and especially **Ellen White** getting on the scoresheet.

BOOM!

Knockout games against **Cameroon** and **Norway** both ended with awesome 3-0 wins for England, including another spectacular strike from **Lucy Bronze** against the Scandinavians.

A USA side in its prime featuring superstars **Megan Rapinoe** and **Alex Morgan** showed their superiority as England were beaten 2-1 in the semi-final.

But , led by Steph Houghton, they more than held their own and showed the world that the **Lionesses** are a footballing force to be reckoned with.

NEXT TIME!

GLOBAL *RIVALS*

ENGLAND'S TOP OPPONENTS IN WORLD FOOTBALL

USA

HONOURS: 4 X WORLD CUPS, 4 X OLYMPIC GOLD
STAR PLAYER: ALEX MORGAN

The USA has long been the **top country** for women's football – the college 'soccer' system has produced some of the world's very best players since the 1980s. Pulling off a win against the USA is a massive achievement for any side in the world!

WHAM!

Alex Morgan

GERMANY

HONOURS: *2 X WORLD CUPS, 8 X EUROS, 1 X OLYMPIC GOLD*

STAR PLAYER: *ALEXANDRA POPP*

Like the men's side, Germany's women are a **footballing powerhouse.** Between 2003 and 2009, they were back-to-back European AND World Champions and remain one of THE sides to beat.

They hadn't conceded a goal at **EURO 2022** until Ella Toone scored against them in the final.

Alexandra Popp

105

SWEDEN

HONOURS: 1 X EURO, 2 X OLYMPIC SILVER
STAR PLAYER: MAGDALENA ERIKSSON

Semi-finalists at the 2019 World Cup, **'The Blue and Yellow'** reached the same stage at EURO 2022, only to be beaten by . . . the **Lionesses**.

FRANCE

HONOURS: -
STAR PLAYER: WENDIE RENARD

Despite lacking major honours, France has always mixed with the best in recent years. Top club sides **Lyon** and **PSG** provide outstanding players for the squad.

SPAIN

HONOURS: 1 X WORLD CUP
STAR PLAYER: ALEXIA PUTELLAS

The newly crowned World Champions are blessed with a talented squad, not least the **2022 Ballon d'Or winner** Alexia Putellas, known for her skills and leadership.

CANADA

HONOURS: 1 X OLYMPIC GOLD
STAR PLAYER: CHRISTINE SINCLAIR

Always in the running in tournaments, thanks in the main to Christine Sinclair, scorer of **190 international goals** – more than any other player, male or female.

BRAZIL

HONOURS: 8 X COPA AMERICAS, 2 X OLYMPIC SILVERS
STAR PLAYER: MARTA

Playing with the same **'samba' style** as the famous men's team, Brazil put on a show, and in Marta - who's played in a record six World Cups - they have a true football legend.

NETHERLANDS

HONOURS: 1 X EURO
STAR PLAYER: VIVIANNE MIEDEMA

Lioness coach **Sarina Wiegman** delivered a EUROs win in 2017 and a place in the World Cup final in 2019, but even without her, this talented squad is a force to be reckoned with.

AUSTRALIA

HONOURS: 1 X ASIAN CUP, 3 X OCEANIAN CUP
STAR PLAYER: SAM KERR

In Sam Kerr, **'The Matildas'** have one of the game's finest talents and after reaching the **World Cup semi-finals** in **2023,** Australia are up there with the best.

JAPAN

HONOURS: 1 X WORLD CUP, 2 X OCEANIAN CUPS, 1 X OLYMPIC SILVER
STAR PLAYER: SAKI KUMAGAI

Japan's **2011 World Cup win** was one of the great football shocks, and they've kept their place in the elite ever since. Captain, **Kumagai** took the winning kick in the final penalty shoot-out.

NORWAY

HONOURS: 1 X WORLD CUP, 1 X EURO, 1 X OLYMPIC GOLD
STAR PLAYER: ADA HEGERBERG

The Scandinavian has a **MASSIVE** history, but has disappointed in recent years, beaten by England (and Lucy Bronze) in two semi-finals. Not to be underestimated though!

DENMARK

HONOURS: -
STAR PLAYER: PERNILLE HARDER

The Danes peaked at **EURO 2017,** beating Germany on their way to their final defeat to the Netherlands. Any team with forward **Pernille Harder** on the pitch is one to be feared.

CHAPTER 9

LIONESSES RULE

SUPER SARINA

POSITION: MIDFIELDER/DEFENDER

CAPS: 99

GOALS: 3

DUTCH CAREER: 1987-2001

NETHERLANDS
ICON

England coach Sarina Wiegman's career as a player began in the USA, with the famed **North Carolina Tar Heels,** where she played  alongside future US icons **Mia Hamm** and **Kristine Lilly.**

POW!

After hanging up her boots, Sarina got her coaching badges and became a hero in her own country, the Netherlands, winning **EURO 2017** and taking the team to the 2019 World Cup final.

England fans couldn't believe their luck when she became manager of the Lionesses in **2021.**

And so, as the **only England football coach** to win a major tournament since the men's team won the World Cup in 1966, **Sarina Wiegman** is an absolute legend . . .

SARINA!
SARINA!
SARINA!

GO, TAR HEELS!

A college football team in the USA, the **UNC Tar Heels** have had a big influence on the success of England's Lionesses.

The Tar Heels are the most successful **US college team ever.** Incredibly, they have been coached by one man - **Anson Dorrance** - since 1979! Many of the current Lionesses have played for the Tar Heels.

The Tar Heels Lionesses:

Sarina Wiegman

Lucy Bronze

Alessia Russo

Lotte Wubben-Moy

Emily Murphy

115

LEAGUE OF SUPER WOMEN

The **Women's Super League** is the top league for women in England. It's where you'll find many of the Lionesses playing their club football . . .

BOOM!

Millie Bright

Lauren James

Fran Kirby

MANCHESTER CITY

Steph Houghton   Alex Greenwood   Chloe Kelly

ARSENAL

Beth Mead   Alessia Russo   Leah Williamson

MANCHESTER UNITED

Ella Toone   Maya Le Tissier   Nikita Parris

TOP TEN *GOALSCORERS*

	PLAYER	YEARS	GOALS
1	Ellen White	*2010–2022*	52
2	Kelly Smith	*1995–2015*	46
3	Kerry Davis	*1982–1998*	44
4=	Karen Walker	*1988–2003*	40
	Fara Williams	*2001–2019*	40
6	Hope Powell	*1983–1998*	35
7	Eniola Aluko	*2004–2017*	33
8	Karen Carney	*2005–2019*	32
9	Gill Coultard	*1981–2000*	30
10	Beth Mead	*2018–*	29

MOST **CAPPED** PLAYERS

	PLAYER	YEARS	CAPS
1	Fara Williams	2001–2019	172
2	Jill Scott	2006–2022	161
3	Karen Carney	2005–2019	144
4	Alex Scott	2004–2017	140
5	Casey Stoney	2000–2018	130
6	Rachel Yankey	1997–2013	129
7	Steph Houghton	2007–	121
8	Gill Coultard	1981–2000	119
9	Kelly Smith	1995–2014	117
10	Ellen White	2010–2022	113

LIONESSES RULE!

We've followed the journey of England's awesome Lionesses – and what a story it is.

They are an inspiration to **millions of young fans** – and have helped take women's football to the stage that it deserves.

This fantastic group of players became **European Champions** and then went all the way to a historic **World Cup Final** in **2023** . . .

WE LOVE YOU ENGLAND!

QUIZ TIME!

How much do you know about the **ENGLAND'S AWESOME LIONESSES?** Try this quiz to find out, then test your friends!

1. For how long did the English FA ban women's football?

----

2. Which team did England play in the first official international?

----

3. Which England manager took the team to the EURO 2009 Final?

----

4. Who is England's most-capped player?

----

5. Who is England's record goalscorer?

----

6. How many goals did England score against Norway at EURO 2022?

----

7. Which player won the EURO 2022 Golden Boot?

----

8. Which Lioness became the world's most expensive female player in 2022?

----

9. With which country did Sarina Wiegman win her first EUROS title?

----

10. Which US college team did Lionesses including Lucy Bronze and Alessia Russo play for?

The answers are on the next page *but no peeking!*

ANSWERS

1. 50 years
2. Scotland
3. Hope Powell
4. Fara Williams
5. Ellen White
6. Eight
7. Beth Mead
8. Keira Walsh
9. The Netherlands
10. University of North Carolina Tar Heels

LIONESSES RULE!

ENGLAND WORDS
YOU NEED TO KNOW

World Cup
The biggest tournament for international teams.

EUROS
The major European tournament for international teams.

Ballon d'Or
The award for the year's best footballer in the world.

Cap
An appearance for international side

WSL
Women's Super League - the top league for women in England

HAVE YOU READ ANY OF THESE OTHER BOOKS FROM THE *SUPERSTARS SERIES?*

FOOTBALL SUPERSTARS

17 FOOTBALL SUPERSTARS
HAALAND
RULES
* FACTS
* STORIES
* STATS
SIMON MUGFORD ★ DAN GREEN

18 FOOTBALL SUPERSTARS
MARTENS
RULES
* FACTS
* STORIES
* STATS
SIMON MUGFORD ★ DAN GREEN

19 FOOTBALL SUPERSTARS
BRONZE
RULES
* FACTS
* STORIES
* STATS
SIMON MUGFORD ★ DAN GREEN

20 FOOTBALL SUPERSTARS
LEWANDOWSKI
RULES
* FACTS
* STORIES
* STATS
SIMON MUGFORD ★ DAN GREEN

GREALISH
RULES
* FACTS
* STORIES
* STATS
SIMON MUGFORD ★ DAN GREEN

22 FOOTBALL SUPERSTARS
FOOTBALL RULES THE WORLD
INCREDIBLE STORIES FROM THE BIGGEST GAME ON THE PLANET
SIMON MUGFORD ★ DAN GREEN

23 FOOTBALL SUPERSTARS
ENGLAND
RULE
* FACTS
* STORIES
* STATS
SIMON MUGFORD ★ DAN GREEN

24 FOOTBALL SUPERSTARS
SAKA
RULES
* FACTS
* STORIES
* STATS
SIMON MUGFORD ★ DAN GREEN

25 FOOTBALL SUPERSTARS
LIONESSES
RULE
* FACTS
* STORIES
* STATS
SIMON MUGFORD ★ DAN GREEN

FOOTBALL SUPERSTARS
FOOTBALL JOKES
RULE
SIMON MUGFORD ★ DAN GREEN

FOOTBALL SUPERSTARS
FOOTBALL QUIZZES
RULE
SIMON MUGFORD ★ DAN GREEN

COLLECT THEM ALL!

SPORTS SUPERSTARS

SPORTS SUPERSTARS
HAMILTON
RULES
* FACTS
* STORIES
* STATS

2 SPORTS SUPERSTARS
RADUCANU
RULES
* FACTS
* STORIES
* STATS
SIMON MUGFORD ★ DAN GREEN

MORE COMING SOON!

ABOUT THE AUTHORS

Simon's first job was at the Science Museum, making paper aeroplanes and blowing bubbles big enough for your dad to stand in. Since then he's written all sorts of books about the stuff he likes, from dinosaurs and rockets, to llamas, loud music and of course, football. Simon has supported Ipswich Town since they won the FA Cup in 1978 (it's true - look it up) and once sat next to Rio Ferdinand on a train. He lives in Kent with his wife and daughter, a dog and a cat.

Dan has drawn silly pictures since he could hold a crayon. Then he grew up and started making books about stuff like trucks, space, people's jobs, *Doctor Who* and *Star Wars*. Dan remembers Ipswich Town winning the FA Cup but he didn't watch it because he was too busy making a Viking ship out of brown paper. As a result, he knows more about Vikings than football. Dan lives in Suffolk with his wife, son, daughter and a dog that takes him for very long walks.

128